Daniel ~
Stand Up Living in a Bow Down World

By
Eric Watt

February 2009
www.ericwatt.com

Copyright © 2009 by Eric Watt

Daniel ~ Stand Up Living in a Bow Down World
by Eric Watt

Printed in the United States of America

ISBN 978-1-60791-678-9

Unless otherwise indicated, Bible quotations are taken from The New International Version of the Bible, Copyright © 1984 by Oxford University Press, and The New Living Translation, Copyright © 1996 by Tyndale House Publishers.

www.xulonpress.com

Introduction

In 530 B.C. there arose a prophet in the Middle East whose integrity, character and inner sensitivity to the Living God shook the entire world. Born into a family of nobility, Daniel was first taken captive and later appointed by a self-promoting, idol-worshipping King to eventually rule over the nation now known as Iran.

What can you and I learn from this Prime Minister from Persia? What about his life can bring hope and clarity in our world? Daniel never compromised with evil, never yielded to peer pressure and never veered off course – completing the destiny God had for him.

We live today in a "bow down" world that is filled with self-promoting leaders and idols of image, stone and self-preservation. We desperately need to be awakened by the message of Daniel, challenged by his courage, and fueled by His God.

For the next 31 days you and I will take a journey back in time and discover the inner strength to be a Daniel in this generation. Each day you will learn a bit of his story, discover practical truths that will build your faith, be given an opportunity to pray to the living God of heaven, and practice Stand Up Living in a Bow Down World!

Let's ask God to help us get started!

Day 1

God Uses Learners

<u>The Story</u>: (Daniel 1:4-20) Captured by King Nebuchadnezzar, Daniel, along with other young men, was selected to be trained in the king's court. Daniel was chosen because he was *"without any physical defect, handsome, showing aptitude for every kind of learning, well-informed, quick to understand and qualified to serve in the king's palace."*

<u>The Truth to Stand On</u>: The king saw in Daniel a unique combination of physical fitness, the desire to serve and a desire to learn. Taken from the comforts of his home in Jerusalem, Daniel was thrown into the uncomfortable position of living with and serving under an evil king. Daniel took the position as a learner and chose to excel among his peers.

<u>Prayer:</u> Dear God, every day I am surrounded by conversations and the lifestyle choices of others that are self-benefitting and not honoring to You. Help me choose not to become like what I hear and see, but to remember that You have placed me here to learn and to listen to Your voice. You have a destiny for me that is greater than my current circumstances! In Jesus' name, Amen.

I will stand up today by…

_____

_____

_____

_____

_____

_____

_____

_____

_____

_____

_____

_____

_____

_____

_____

_____

_____

_____

_____

Day 2

Choose Not to be Defiled by the World

<u>The Story:</u> (Daniel 1:4-20) The food offered to Daniel and his friends was the best in the land, filled with the choicest of meat and drink – but it had been offered to idols. Rather than seek the approval of the king, the king's servants and his peers, Daniel *"resolved not to defile himself with the royal food and wine, and he asked the chief official for permission not to defile himself in this way."*

<u>The Truth to Stand On</u>: Every day Daniel was faced with choices that would shape his destiny. Not content to compromise with the idolatrous practices of the king and his peers, Daniel let his employer know that he chose a different way. He didn't ridicule those around him that did not know God, but he did commit that at all costs he would not defile his spirit or his body.

<u>Prayer:</u> Dear Heavenly Father, today I am choosing you over "fitting in" with my peers and those in authority over me. I ask that you give me strength to not defile my own heart and body even with the small matters like what I eat, drink, watch, listen to and speak about. I choose You, knowing that Your ways are higher and better than those around me. In Jesus' name, Amen.

I will stand up today by…

_____

_____

_____

_____

_____

_____

_____

_____

_____

_____

_____

_____

_____

_____

_____

_____

_____

_____

_____

Day 3

God Brings Favor to His Children

The Story: (Daniel 1:4-20) Daniel's conviction not to compromise or eat the royal food had the potential for creating devastating, life-ending consequences for both himself and his employer. It was a risk worth taking because God is a God worth serving. What happens next in the story is truly amazing – God directly intervenes on Daniel's behalf. *"Now God had caused the official to show favor and sympathy to Daniel."*

The Truth to Stand On: Daniel's righteous behavior and convictions not to eat the king's food came from an intimate relationship with the eternal God. He valued his ongoing relationship with the Creator more than life itself. In fact, this decision put Daniel in a place of vulnerability. However, God's response to Daniel's boldness was immediate and complete. God confirmed His covenant by extending favor in Daniel's workplace.

Prayer: Lord, You are dependable and unchanging. I can trust You to care for every part of my life. Today I will step out of the "comforts" of my surroundings and into a place of conviction and righteous behavior. I know that as I use my faith to step out like Daniel did, you will confirm your covenant favor in my life. In Jesus' name, Amen.

I will stand up today by…

_____

_____

_____

_____

_____

_____

_____

_____

_____

_____

_____

_____

_____

_____

_____

_____

_____

_____

_____

Day 4

God Blesses Those Who Honor Him

<u>The Story:</u> (Daniel 1:4-20) Daniel's boldness confirmed again that God always fulfills His covenant with those whose lives are obedient and faithful. For ten days Daniel and His friends chose God rather than the best the world around them had to offer. It was not a contest pitting colleague against colleague or friend against friend. This was an opportunity for God to make His name known in the earth. What happened? *"At the end of ten days they looked healthier and better nourished than any of the young men who ate the royal food."*

<u>The Truth to Stand On:</u> When we choose to be put to the test for God, we must depend only on God and not on the circumstances around us. During the ten days that Daniel was tested he waited on God and did not intervene. It was God's turn to bless, and Daniel did not need to interfere or waiver in his faith. God is faithful to His WORD.

<u>Prayer:</u> Heavenly Father and Ruler of All, I have stepped out today to live a "Daniel" life. I am asking to be tested and found with Your favor. I know that you promise to accompany my life with blessings (Deuteronomy 28:2) when I obey you, so I ask for courage today to step out beyond my peers and see You do what only You can do. In Jesus' name, Amen.

I will stand up today by…

_____

_____

_____

_____

_____

_____

_____

_____

_____

_____

_____

_____

_____

_____

_____

_____

_____

_____

_____

Day 5

God Imparts Wisdom, Knowledge and Understanding

The Story: (Daniel 1:4-20) Daniel and his friends trusted God to make a difference in their lives. It was a move of surrender that yielded success. By choosing and remaining in God's ways, Daniel automatically qualified for a supernatural impartation from heaven. *"To these four young men God gave knowledge and understanding of all kinds of literature and learning. And Daniel could understand visions and dreams of all kinds."*

The Truth to Stand On: Daniel chose to be tested for God and God chose to reveal his wisdom, knowledge and understanding. What an amazing covenant agreement Daniel had with the living God! Daniel never pitted his own wisdom against that of his peers, he drew from the resources of heaven so that God might be glorified. God seeks out "Daniels" in every generation who will yield the right of way to God's unlimited wisdom and understanding.

Prayer: Eternal God of wisdom and strength, today I am going to take "Daniel" steps toward a yielded and surrendered life. I can see that Your nature is to impart the supernatural to those who are wholly dependant on you. Give me courage to stop depending on my own strength and to expect your wisdom and revelation. In this way those around me will see that You are great and glorious. In Jesus' name, Amen.

I will stand up today by…

_____

_____

_____

_____

_____

_____

_____

_____

_____

_____

_____

_____

_____

_____

_____

_____

_____

_____

_____

_____

Day 6

God Causes His Children to Succeed

The Story: (Daniel 1:4-20) Daniel and his friends were put to the test in the king's chambers on the king's terms. They were questioned and compared to the other students who drew from the traditions and spiritual insight of the day. It was a pass/fail test and they passed. *"In every matter of wisdom and understanding about which the king questioned them, he found them ten times better than all the magicians and enchanters in his whole kingdom."*

The Truth to Stand On: Daniel and his friends chose to be tested, but could not dictate the timing or the nature of the test. But, God who is infinite in wisdom has already pre-determined that those who rely on Him will be given answers, solutions and insight by His Spirit. They were 10 times wiser and stronger than their peers!

Prayer: Heavenly Father, when I am called to be tested I will trust You! You will make available the resources of heaven to honor Your name. Help me today to fix my eyes steadily on you so that I can see Your miracle-working love at work. In Jesus' name, Amen.

I will stand up today by…

_____

_____

_____

_____

_____

_____

_____

_____

_____

_____

_____

_____

_____

_____

_____

_____

_____

_____

Day 7

Worshipping a False God is Idolatry

<u>The Story:</u> (Daniel 3:1-25) When King Nebuchadnezzar erected an idol of gold and summoned the people to bow down in worship; he created a crisis of belief for every follower of God. To worship an "image" was in direct conflict to the 3rd commandment, but to not worship the idol was to bring on the death sentence. There was no middle ground. *"Whoever does not fall down and worship will immediately be thrown into a blazing furnace."*

<u>The Truth to Stand On:</u> Well meaning leaders and people of influence often create "images" for others to follow. The king went to great lengths to organize the construction of an idol and the worship of his god. Then he commanded everyone to bow down and pay allegiance to this false image. Any image made by human hands or crafted by human ingenuity stands in direct contradiction to God's command to not bow down to any image.

<u>Prayer:</u> Creator God, You alone are the one true God. There are so many influences around me promoting larger than life entertainment, sports and political heroes. When the crowds begin to change their behavior and their clothes to become like these idols, grant me the strength to desire to please You and You alone. If it costs me everything, I will not bow down. In Jesus' name, Amen.

I will stand up today by…

_____

_____

_____

_____

_____

_____

_____

_____

_____

_____

_____

_____

_____

_____

_____

_____

_____

Day 8

Self-Defense Doesn't Honor God

<u>The Story:</u> (Daniel 3:1-25) Furious with rage the king summoned the three young men who refused to bow their knees and hearts to the idol. He questioned their loyalty to his kingdom and then threatened them with death by fire. These godly men not only did not bow down, but they refused to act in self-defense. *"O Nebuchadnezzar, we do not need to defend ourselves before you in this matter."*

<u>The Truth to Stand On:</u> Shadrach, Meshach and Abednego stood up for God when the world around them was bowing down. By not bending their knees to the false image they incurred the wrath of their employer and king. Even more, they chose to value the living God more than their own lives. When challenged by the king they openly admitted their allegiance to God.

<u>Prayer:</u> Dear Father, Grant me the strength today to withstand the pressures to lessen my convictions in order to fit in with those whose hearts and knees are bowing down to false images and idols of power. I will choose you and will resist the temptation to draw attention to myself through self-defense. Worshipping You and You alone is worth it! In Jesus' name, Amen.

I will stand up today by…

_____

_____

_____

_____

_____

_____

_____

_____

_____

_____

_____

_____

_____

_____

_____

_____

_____

_____

Day 9

God is a Savior

The Story: (Daniel 3:1-25) King Nebuchadnezzar threatened the three young leaders with death by fire for refusing to bow to an idol. Without hesitation they did not cower or attempt to convince the king of their innocence. Instead they declared, *"If we are thrown into the blazing furnace, the God we serve is able to save us from it, and he will rescue us from your hand, O King."*

The Truth to Stand On: God is a Savior to those who choose Him! In the face of incredible pressure to conform and to yield to the power of their king, the three young rulers stood strong and declared their allegiance to God. Whether removed from the flames or killed by the fire their faith was fixed on a Savior who would rescue them from the hand of the king.

Prayer: Lord and Savior, today I choose you. In the face of peer pressure to conform, to bow down and worship the idols of this world, I commit to remain strong and wait for your salvation. However you choose to move in my life, I will accept your rescue from the enemy. In Jesus' name, Amen.

I will stand up today by...

_____

_____

_____

_____

_____

_____

_____

_____

_____

_____

_____

_____

_____

_____

_____

_____

_____

_____

Day 10

God is Sovereign

<u>The Story:</u> (Daniel 3:1-25) Threatened to be thrown into the fiery furnace, Shadrach, Meshach and Abednego chose to leave their future to God rather than take matters into their own hands. They were not tempted by the offer of a compromise. In fact, their resolve and boldness toward King Nebuchadnezzar brought clarity in the midst of a huge crisis. *"But even if He does not [save us], we want you to know, O king, that we will not serve your gods or worship the image of gold you have set up."*

<u>The Truth to Stand On:</u> God is Sovereign and can be completely trusted. The three young men were faced with a bigger choice than standing up or bowing down. Who would be responsible for their eternity? An image crafted by the most skilled man can not compare to the Creator of men. There was no real choice to be made. God is God.

<u>Prayer:</u> Dear Heavenly Father, I ask for the strength today to not compromise. The world around me offers its short-term pleasure but demands long-term allegiance. You alone, God, are worthy of my allegiance, and I will trust my day and my future into Your hands. In Jesus' name, Amen.

I will stand up today by…

_____

_____

_____

_____

_____

_____

_____

_____

_____

_____

_____

_____

_____

_____

_____

_____

_____

Day 11

Worshipping God is Costly

The Story: (Daniel 3:1-25) Shadrach, Meshach and Abednego had declared their allegiance to the living God and were ready to endure whatever consequences would come their way. They had sealed their future in God. King Nebuchadnezzar was furious at their righteous response. *"Then Nebuchadnezzar was furious with Shadrach, Meshach and Abednego, and his attitude toward them changed. He ordered the furnace heated seven times hotter than usual."*

The Truth to Stand On: Declaring their allegiance to God and not the king secured these three young rulers' eternity. But it did not remove them from the current crisis. When the king ordered the furnace to be turned up, these young men had perhaps one last chance to compromise their faith and live. The consequences of their convictions were to cost them everything.

Prayer: Heavenly Father, I realize that choosing to worship You creates a peace in my own heart that can withstand the pressures of the world around me. Having You with me now and forever is a far greater prize than the approval of others around me. Grant to me today the courage to choose You, even when the impact of my decision seems costly. In Jesus' name, Amen.

I will stand up today by…

_____

_____

_____

_____

_____

_____

_____

_____

_____

_____

_____

_____

_____

_____

_____

_____

_____

_____

_____

Day 12

Your Enemy is For Your Destruction

<u>The Story:</u> (Daniel 3:1-25) King Nebuchadnezzar followed through on his promise and commanded his strongest soldiers to tie up and throw Shadrach, Meshach and Abednego into the fiery furnace. Nebuchadnezzar had his own interests in mind and saw these three men as expendable. He *"commanded some of the strongest soldiers in his army to tie [them up] and throw them into the blazing furnace."*

<u>The Truth to Stand On:</u> The king and his soldiers were not neutral in their attitudes and actions toward Shadrach, Meshach and Abednego. They were real enemies of God, His servants and His eternal kingdom. In the mind of the king no punishment was too great to keep "control" of his subjects.

<u>Prayer:</u> O Great and Eternal King, today I can see my own life being lived out amidst people whose intentions are not for You, Your servants and Your kingdom. Like the three young rulers, I also live in a spiritual war. Grant to me the grace to respond to the battle with strength from You, never seeking to harm those whose eyes have not been opened to Your mercy and love. In Jesus' name, Amen.

I will stand up today by…

_____

_____

_____

_____

_____

_____

_____

_____

_____

_____

_____

_____

_____

_____

_____

_____

_____

_____

Day 13

God is Trustworthy

The Story: (Daniel 3:1-25) The soldiers who bound and threw Shadrach, Meshach and Abednego into the fire perished in the flames. But the young rulers landed in the furnace unbound and unharmed. They were supernaturally protected and joined by God himself. The king said, *"Look, I see four men walking around in the fire, unbound, unharmed, and the fourth looks like a son of the gods."*

The Truth to Stand On: When Shadrach, Meshach and Abednego were thrown into the fire the only expectation they had was to be in God's presence. Unsure of their future, they were certain of their destiny. They survived the fiery crisis by the very real and tangible presence of God in their midst.

Prayer: Dear Heavenly Father, I am so grateful that You are with me in times of trial. Today, as I step into the "fires" around me I can expect Your presence to surround me and to keep me from harm. Because You are trustworthy in every circumstance, I place my future into Your hands. In Jesus' name, Amen.

I will stand up today by...

_____

_____

_____

_____

_____

_____

_____

_____

_____

_____

_____

_____

_____

_____

_____

_____

_____

Day 14

You Live in a Spiritual Battle

The Story: (Daniel 3:18-28) To the natural eye Shadrach, Meshach and Abednego resisted pressure from the king and refused to bow down to a pagan idol. But there is much more to the story. These three young men were engaged in a spiritual battle that turned the king to rage. *"Then Nebuchadnezzar was furious with Shadrach, Meshach and Abednego, and his attitude toward them changed. He ordered the furnace heated seven times hotter than usual."*

The Truth to Stand On: There was no doubt in the minds of these three young rulers. Standing up for God meant standing against the ruling spiritual powers of the day. Their convictions to do right and to live right turned up the heat against them. This is standing operating procedure in the spiritual realm. A stand for God is a choice to engage in the battle!

Prayer: Dear Heavenly Father, Today I am standing on the convictions of Your Word and stepping into the spiritual battle. I ask that you would guide and protect me each step of the way as I learn to depend on you. In Jesus' name, Amen.

I will stand up today by...

_____

_____

_____

_____

_____

_____

_____

_____

_____

_____

_____

_____

_____

_____

_____

_____

_____

Day 15

Your Enemy Will Self-Destruct

<u>The Story:</u> (Daniel 3:18-28) God is in charge of your spiritual battle and, no matter how bad it looks, good will come of it. As the three young rulers were hauled off to the fire, the forces of evil self-destruction began to overcome the king and his soldiers. *"The king's command was urgent and the furnace so hot that the flames of the fire killed the soldiers who took up Shadrach, Meshach and Abednego and these three men, firmly tied, fell into the blazing fire."*

<u>The Truth to Stand On:</u> Shadrach, Meshach and Abednego, headed to what they presumed was their death; instead they watched the enemy surrounding them die. It was a signal from heaven and a clue about the future. God's people are protected from the wrath of self-destruction; and God always makes Himself known to those in the fire.

<u>Prayer:</u> Dear Heavenly Father, Your Word instructs me to "stand still and see the salvation of the Lord" (Exodus 14:13-14). Today I choose to stand and watch Your salvation overtake my circumstances. Grant me the courage to not waiver or cower in the battle so that I can see Your victory in my life. In Jesus' name, Amen.

I will stand up today by…

_____

_____

_____

_____

_____

_____

_____

_____

_____

_____

_____

_____

_____

_____

_____

_____

_____

_____

Day 16

Seekers Will Find God

The Story: (Daniel 3:18-28) Panic must have overtaken King Nebuchadnezzar as he watched his best soldiers die near the furnace and Shadrach, Meshach and Abednego live. His own attempts to crush these young rulers did not have the strength to overcome a true and living God. This opened the king's eyes. *"Then King Nebuchadnezzar leapt to his feet in amazement and asked his advisers, 'Weren't there three men that we tied up and threw into the fire?'."*

The Truth to Stand On: God has a purpose in the fiery furnace. The king mustered his best soldiers together and turned up the fire in the furnace, but it was still not enough to intimidate the true and living God. It was in the midst of this attack the king learned that he was no match for the one, true God.

Prayer: Dear Father, Help me to stay strong and to never waiver in the battle. When I stand up in the convictions of Your Word the power of Your name is showcased to those who oppose Your ways. Today, I ask that You keep me strong, and that You reveal yourself to those who oppose you. In Jesus' name, Amen.

I will stand up today by…

_____

_____

_____

_____

_____

_____

_____

_____

_____

_____

_____

_____

_____

_____

_____

_____

_____

Day 17

God Dwells with His Servants

The Story: (Daniel 3:18-28) To his own shock King Nebuchadnezzar was not able to control his own power or destiny. He was bested by the King of Kings. He threw Shadrach, Meshach and Abednego into the fiery furnace but never expected them to be joined by the living God! *"Look, I see four men walking around in the fire, unbound, unharmed, and the fourth looks like a son of the gods."*

The Truth to Stand On: The king learned an incredible lesson. His idol had no real power. As he watched his own soldiers die and the bindings come off his prisoners as they fell into the blaze, the fiery furnace served as an invitation for a divine guest. God is present with His own when they are thrown into the fire.

Prayer: Dear Father, as I face my own "fire" today, I will not shrink from difficulty, pain or suffering. Instead, I will look for you in the midst of it. You will come and dwell with me and show Yourself strong! In Jesus' name, Amen.

I will stand up today by…

_____

_____

_____

_____

_____

_____

_____

_____

_____

_____

_____

_____

_____

_____

_____

_____

_____

_____

_____

Day 18

God Rescues His Children

<u>The Story:</u> (Daniel 3:18-28) When the king's world crumbled he was able to see the Most High God. His best plans to force others to bow down to a false idol had been foiled by three young rulers who chose God instead of temporary comfort. In the end, even the king acknowledged the great rescue. *"Nebuchadnezzar then approached the opening of the blazing furnace and shouted, 'Shadrach, Meshach and Abednego, servants of the Most High God, come out!'."*

<u>The Truth to Stand On:</u> God never abandons His children. Faced with the greatest test of their lives, Shadrach, Meshach and Abednego put their future in God's hands, and God came to rescue them in the fire. In the end, these young rulers had an encounter with God, and the king received revelation.

<u>Prayer:</u> Heavenly Father, You are the Most High God! I praise You today that the authority of Your name is above every other name. I ask that You reveal Yourself to those who oppose me and that you rescue me in the midst of my trials. In Jesus' name, Amen.

I will stand up today by…

_____

_____

_____

_____

_____

_____

_____

_____

_____

_____

_____

_____

_____

_____

_____

_____

Day 19

God Carries Pain for His Children

<u>The Story:</u> (Daniel 18-28) God not only rescued Shadrach, Meshach and Abednego in the midst of their fire, but He took their pain upon himself. There is no other explanation for these young rulers to come out of the fire unscathed than the words of the prophet Isaiah: "surely He took up our infirmities and carried our sorrows". *"They saw that the fire had not harmed their bodies, nor was a hair of their heads singed; their robes were not scorched, and there was no smell of fire on them."*

<u>The Truth to Stand On:</u> King Nebuchadnezzar and his men were stunned when the three young rulers came out of the fiery furnace completely untouched by the fire. The blaze had killed the king's best, but it could not touch God's anointed. God descended and dwelled among these men and had taken their pain. He always defends His own.

<u>Prayer:</u> Dear Father, I trust You. Even when unfortunate circumstances and difficulties come my way You are the one that I will turn to. You are dependable and trustworthy; and you will rescue me in the fire. I know that You have already taken the long-term scars of suffering from me so that I can rejoice with You in times of trial. God I trust you! Amen.

I will stand up today by…

_____

_____

_____

_____

_____

_____

_____

_____

_____

_____

_____

_____

_____

_____

_____

_____

Day 20

God Receives the Glory

The Story: (Daniel 3:18-28) King Nebuchadnezzar turns from being the opposition to being an endorser of the true and living God. Astounded at the miracle of God's intervention the king honors God and the three young rulers. *"Praise be to the God of Shadrach, Meshach, and Abednego, who has sent his angel and rescued his servants! They trusted in Him, defied the king's command and were willing to give up their lives rather than serve or worship any god except their own God."*

The Truth to Stand On: The conviction to stand strong in the midst of the battle and the overwhelming presence of God always combine for a miracle. The evil king ceases to bow down to his lifeless idol and praises the true God. He also honors the three young rulers whose convictions brought them through the fire.

Prayer: Dear Heavenly Father, I am convinced that You will show Yourself strong when I stand strong for You. Help me to never forget that You delight in rescuing Your children and in revealing Your purposes to those who seek You. Use me today, even in the fire, to bring others to praise Your name. In Jesus' name, Amen.

I will stand up today by…

_____

_____

_____

_____

_____

_____

_____

_____

_____

_____

_____

_____

_____

_____

_____

_____

_____

_____

_____

Day 21

God Judges Good and Evil

The Story: (Daniel 5:1-31) The son of Nebuchadnezzar, Belshazzar, had become king but chose not to follow his father's late-in-life commitment to the one true God. He threw a great banquet for his nobles, wives and mistresses. As the king and his party drank from the gold and silver goblets stolen from the temple in Jerusalem they praised the idols of their day. God's judgment was on the way! *"Suddenly the fingers of a human hand appeared and wrote on the plaster of the wall."*

The Truth to Stand On: You and I can have confidence that we are not alone in this world. God is always watching over His word to see that it is carried out (Jeremiah 1:12). King Belshazzar's brazen worship of idols with goblets from God's temple brought the hand of God into the room!

Prayer: Dear Heavenly Father, I will walk in confident faith today, knowing that You are near me and that You are making sure that Your Word is at work in the circumstances of my life. I trust you to intervene and to judge the good and the evil that surrounds me. I will look for Your hand to be evident in my life. In Jesus' name, Amen.

I will stand up today by…

_____

_____

_____

_____

_____

_____

_____

_____

_____

_____

_____

_____

_____

_____

_____

_____

_____

Day 22

God Ordains Your Work

<u>The Story:</u> (Daniel 5:1-31) When God's hand appeared and wrote something that the king couldn't understand, Belshazzar was terrified! He called out the best astrologers, enchanters and diviners of the day to interpret the message, but they were baffled. Then the queen remembered and called for Daniel. *"There is a man in your kingdom who has the spirit of the holy gods in him. In the time of your father he was found to have insight and intelligence and wisdom like that of the gods. He also had the ability to interpret dreams – call for Daniel and he will tell you what the writing means."*

<u>The Truth to Stand On:</u> During the reign of King Belshazzar Daniel was forgotten. No longer in the king's court, Daniel had been pushed aside. But when difficulty came God's people are remembered for who they are and for what God can do through them.

<u>Prayer:</u> God who made the Heavens, I am grateful that You have promised to never leave or forsake me. Even when those around me seem to have forgotten, I know that You have a plan to reveal Yourself to them. Use me today to showcase Your amazing love, mercy and truth. In Jesus' Name, Amen.

I will stand up today by…

_____

_____

_____

_____

_____

_____

_____

_____

_____

_____

_____

_____

_____

_____

_____

_____

_____

_____

Day 23

God Builds Character

<u>The Story:</u> (Daniel 5:1-31) The king and his counsel could not solve the mystery of the handwriting on the wall, and in total desperation he orders his soldiers to go and find Daniel. The king says to Daniel: *"I have heard that the spirit of the gods is in you and that you have insight, intelligence and outstanding wisdom."*

<u>The Truth to Stand On:</u> Taken from obscurity and brought back to the king's palace, Daniel was remembered for the imprint of God in his life. Above all those who gave counsel to the king's father, Daniel was known for his relationship with the true and living God and for the consistency of his righteous character.

<u>Prayer:</u> Lord, I ask today that You place Your imprint in my life so that others will see Your work in my life. Transform my character so that Your influence through me becomes evident to all. In Jesus' name, Amen.

I will stand up today by…

_____

_____

_____

_____

_____

_____

_____

_____

_____

_____

_____

_____

_____

_____

_____

_____

Day 24

God Always Receives the Glory

<u>The Story:</u> (Daniel 5:1-31) King Belshazzar offers a significant reward to Daniel if he can interpret the handwriting. But Daniel is only interested in receiving affirmation and accolades from the Heavenly King and instead declares: *"You may keep your gifts for yourself and give your rewards to someone else. Nevertheless, I will read the writing for the king and tell him what it means."*

<u>The Truth to Stand On:</u> The giving and receiving of rewards for a job well done is a natural part of life. But Daniel realizes that the king intends to honor him rather than God when the interpretation was given, so he deflects the rewards and makes it very clear that God alone is the one who grants wisdom.

<u>Prayer:</u> Dear Heavenly Father, there is a temptation to claim credit for the things that You alone can create. Teach me today to be like Daniel – faithful to excellence in effort, but never claiming credit for the results. You alone deserve all the praise. For by You, through You and in You all things have been created (Romans 11:36). In Jesus' name, Amen.

I will stand up today by…

_____

_____

_____

_____

_____

_____

_____

_____

_____

_____

_____

_____

_____

_____

_____

_____

_____

_____

_____

Day 25

God is in Control of the Circumstances

<u>The Story:</u> (Daniel 5:1-31) When God granted the king's father great power, responsibility and authority he became arrogant and full of pride instead of honoring the true and living God. God's response to his ungrateful and rebellious heart? Nebuchadnezzar *"was driven away from people and given the mind of an animal; he lived with wild donkeys and ate grass like cattle...until he acknowledged that the Most High God is sovereign over the kingdoms of men."*

<u>The Truth to Stand On:</u> Actions have consequences and the king's father was no exception. When the king's father refused to acknowledge God, his life was drastically altered. For seven years he lived and ate among animals and then, once he repented, God restored his kingdom. But his son, King Belshazzar, never learned from his father's painful experience.

<u>Prayer:</u> Dear heavenly Father, today I acknowledge that You are in control of every circumstance. Help me to never ignore Your handiwork in my life. Instead, from now on I will choose to give thanks in every circumstance being grateful for Your blessings and direction in my life. In Jesus' name, Amen.

I will stand up today by…

_____

_____

_____

_____

_____

_____

_____

_____

_____

_____

_____

_____

_____

_____

_____

_____

Day 26

God Orders Your Day

The Story: (Daniel 5:1-31) The king had no idea that Daniel's words would describe his doom. Because of King Belshazzar's rebellion his own life was about to end. *"But you did not honor the God who holds in His hand your life and all your ways. Therefore He sent the hand that wrote the inscription."*

The Truth to Stand On: God holds in His hands the life of every person. For the arrogant and ungodly King Belshazzar there was to be no future. The hand writing on the wall – Mene, Mene, Tekel, Peres – meant God was bringing an end to Belshazzar's rule, that his life was found wanting and his successor would be his enemy. God is not to be mocked, because every person will reap a destiny based on their actions (Galatians 6:7).

The Prayer: Dear Father in heaven, You alone hold the world and all that is in it. You determine the beginning and the end of my life, the circumstances in which I live and the purpose for which I am born. I come humbly to You today asking for wisdom and guidance to live right in your eyes. In Jesus' name, Amen.

I will stand up today by…

_____

_____

_____

_____

_____

_____

_____

_____

_____

_____

_____

_____

_____

_____

_____

_____

_____

_____

Day 27

God's Word is True

The Story: (Daniel 5:1-31) When Daniel finished interpreting the writing on the wall the king commanded that the royal cloth and a gold chain be placed around his neck, making him the third highest ruler in the kingdom. But Belshazzar's actions were feeble in the face of an all powerful God. *"That very night Belshazzar, king of the Babylonians, was slain."*

The Truth to Stand On: Even when the indictment was read by Daniel the king tried to maintain control by granting Daniel the very things he didn't desire. But it was the king's last act. The fulfillment of the prophetic words on the wall had immediate impact. The king was slain and the kingdom was given over to the enemy.

Prayer: Dear Father, Your words are unchanging. Whatever You say is true and worth more than life itself. Today I will choose to obey and humble myself to walk in covenant obedience to You. I put my future in Your hands. In Jesus' name, Amen.

I will stand up today by…

_____

_____

_____

_____

_____

_____

_____

_____

_____

_____

_____

_____

_____

_____

_____

_____

_____

_____

Day 28

God Rewards Integrity

The Story: (Daniel 6:1-23) In 522 BC, at the age of sixty two, the Kurdish leader Darius became king of what is now Iran. He immediately appointed 123 officials to help govern the kingdom. The prophet Daniel quickly rose to the top of the list and was about to be promoted to be the Prime Minister. *"Now Daniel so distinguished himself among [his peers] by his exceptional qualities that the king planned to set him over the whole kingdom."*

Truth to Stand On: The character and excellence of Daniel was unsurpassed in the kingdom. As the king was about to reward him, his colleagues became jealous and attempted to find a flaw that would end his career. But God's work in Daniel was so strong that they could find nothing wrong. God rewards integrity.

Prayer: Dear heavenly Father, I ask that you would put in me the same kind of integrity and excellence that promoted Daniel far beyond his peers. I know that this may cause a reaction of jealousy among my peers; and, if it does, I ask that you would grant me the strength of character to stand strong. In Jesus' name, Amen.

I will stand up today by…

_____

_____

_____

_____

_____

_____

_____

_____

_____

_____

_____

_____

_____

_____

_____

_____

_____

_____

Day 29

God and His Servants Are Inseparable

The Story: (Daniel 6:1-23) Daniel's character and reputation caught the attention of his employer, and he was set apart from his peers. Jealous colleagues then devised an evil plot to destroy Daniel's life. But God was on the side of Daniel. They could find no corruption in him and said: *"we will never find any basis for charges against this man Daniel unless it has something to do with the law of his God."*

The Truth to Stand On: A righteous, yet humble, character and a reputation for excellence are qualities that established Daniel in his job. But both the king and his peers saw in Daniel more than excellence, there was an inseparable covenant relationship between God and this leader. When God makes covenant with His people he never leaves them.

The Prayer: Dear heavenly Father, today I ask that you would establish Your covenant in my life and in my family. I want to be known as a person who stands for You, with You and in You. Do whatever it takes to make Yourself known through me. In Jesus' name, Amen.

I will stand up today by…

_____

_____

_____

_____

_____

_____

_____

_____

_____

_____

_____

_____

_____

_____

_____

_____

_____

_____

Day 30

God Honors Faithfulness and Hears Our Prayers

<u>The Story:</u> (Daniel 6:1-23) Daniel responds to the new decree to worship the earthly king by not changing his routine. He must have known that others were watching his every move. He returned to his home, opened his window so that all could hear and knelt down to pray to God. *"Three times a day he got down on his knees and prayed, giving thanks to God, just as he had done before and asked God for help."*

<u>The Truth to Stand On:</u> The pressure to conform to a lower standard can be immense, especially when the consequences of maintaining integrity are costly. Daniel made a conscious decision to not be swayed, and God honored him for it.

<u>The Prayer:</u> Dear Lord, You are my strength today. I am choosing to not bow down to peer pressure or to be swayed by compromise. I will instead cling to a pattern of humble submission to You as the true and living God. I place my day and my future in Your hands. In Jesus' name, Amen.

I will stand up today by...

_____

_____

_____

_____

_____

_____

_____

_____

_____

_____

_____

_____

_____

_____

_____

_____

_____

_____

Day 31

God is a Deliverer

<u>The Story:</u> (Daniel 6:1-23) Daniel was thrown into the lions' den and a stone was placed over its mouth. There was no escape. It was a miserably long night for the king as he thought of the eternal destiny of his trusted servant. Early the next morning the king rushed to the lions' den and called out, *"Daniel, servant of the living God, has your God, whom you serve continually, been able to rescue you from the lions? Daniel answered, 'My God sent his angel and He shut the mouths of the lions. They have not hurt me because I was found innocent in His sight'."*

<u>The Truth to Stand On:</u> King Darius could not stop the mouths of his servants from turning against his Prime Minister, but God shut the mouths of the lions! Daniel was delivered because of his innocence and not wounded because he placed his trust in God.

<u>The Prayer:</u> You God, are my Deliverer! I will trust in You today and not be ashamed. Even when the enemy could devour me, I will remain at peace in Your presence. You are to be praised, for You are great and mighty to save. In Jesus' name, Amen.

I will stand up today by…

_____

_____

_____

_____

_____

_____

_____

_____

_____

_____

_____

_____

_____

_____

_____

_____

_____

_____

_____

_____

Conclusion

You and I have begun an incredible journey together. For the past 31 days we have lived, breathed and prayed through the life of Daniel. Inspired by Daniel's example and courage, you are well on your way to practice Stand Up Living in a Bow Down World! God will be your source of strength and your foundation in the days ahead.

Our world is crippled by weak-kneed leaders and desperately needs to see a "Daniel" living out his or her faith in the midst of perilous times. This is your moment, your season to be strong in the power of His might.

It is my prayer that God, who is full of mercy and never-ending kindness will find you faithful and strong to the very end.

Eric Watt

Breinigsville, PA USA
22 September 2009
224491BV00001B/1/P

9 781607 916789